Wildly Weird Weather
Gareth Stevens
PUBLISHING
I0817101
IT'S NOT SUPPOSED TO SNOW HERE!
By Jill Keppeler

Please visit our website, www.garethstevens.com. For a free color catalog of all our high-quality books, call toll free 1-800-542-2595 or fax 1-877-542-2596.

Cataloging-in-Publication Data

Names: Keppeler, Jill.
Title: It's Not Supposed to Snow Here!/ Jill Keppeler.
Description: New York : Gareth Stevens Publishing, 2024. | Series: Wildly weird weather | Includes glossary and index.
Identifiers: ISBN 9781538287972 (pbk.) | ISBN 9781538287989 (library bound) | ISBN 9781538287996 (ebook)
Subjects: LCSH: Snow–Juvenile literature. | Snow–Miscellanea–Juvenile literature.
Classification: LCC QC926.37 K44 2024 | DDC 551.57'84 –dc23

First Edition

Published in 2024 by
Gareth Stevens Publishing
2544 Clinton St.
Buffalo, NY 14224

Designer: Corinne Eberwine
Editor: Theresa Emminizer

Photo credits: Cover, LHBLLC/Shutterstock.com; p. 5 Pressmaster/Shutterstock.com; p. 6 Mariia Tagirova/Shutterstock.com; p. 7 Miramiska/Shutterstock.com; p. 9 Dale Lorna Jacobsen/Shutterstock.com; p. 10 John Dvorak/Shutterstock.com; p. 13 Julien Hautcoeur/Shutterstock.com; p. 14 VectorMine/Shutterstock.com; p 17 (inset) Nook Hok/Shutterstock.com; p. 17 Shaheem Sutherland/Shutterstock.com; p. 18 Jimmy Rooney/Shutterstock.com; p. 21 Africa Studio/Shutterstock.com.

Printed in the United States of America

CPSIA compliance information: Batch #CS24GS: For further information contact Gareth Stevens, New York, New York at 1-800-542-2595.

CONTENTS

Words in the glossary appear in **bold** type the first time they are used in the text.

WHAT IS THIS!?

In some parts of the world, it's not strange at all to wake up in the morning and look out your window to a world of white—everything covered in snow. However, in many other places, this would be a huge surprise. You might think: "It's not supposed to snow here! What's going on?"

But snow is a type of **precipitation** that can happen in some surprising places and at some surprising times. It just takes the right conditions to create that world of white!

Snow can be a lot of fun! However, it can also cause problems.

SCIENCE OF SNOW

Snow isn't just frozen rain. It's precipitation made up of tiny ice crystals. It may be made of single crystals or many crystals stuck together in snowflakes. These crystals form in the clouds from water vapor if it's cold enough—about 32°F (0°C) and lower.

A single snowflake may have up to 100 ice crystals. No two snowflakes will be exactly the same!

ice crystals

Heavier ice crystals fall to the ground by themselves or as snowflakes. It must be cold in the clouds and near the ground for the snow to reach the earth.

Most snowflakes have six sides or points. This depends on how their crystals join together.

SNOW NEEDS WATER

Lower **temperatures** alone aren't enough to cause snow in an area. There must also be a certain amount of humidity. Humidity is moisture, or water, in the air. Without this moisture, there's nothing to form the ice crystals that make up snowflakes.

Antarctica is Earth's southernmost **continent.** It's very cold, but it's also very dry. This lack of humidity means it doesn't snow much. However, the snow that does fall in Antarctica hardly ever melts. It turns into ice.

Much of Antarctica is covered in a huge sheet of ice. However, the continent's "dry valleys" are areas without ice where snow almost never falls.

Some of the coldest places in the world don't usually get snow. This is because of a lack of humidity. Many deserts can be very cold at night, but they're also very dry. There's no moisture to create snow.

SURPRISE SNOWFALL

Because snow needs cold air in which to form, many people think warmer places never get snow at all. However, this often isn't true! Even in warm places the conditions sometimes line up and snow can form.

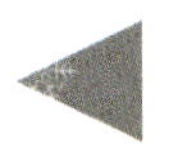

In February 2019, parts of Los Angeles got a dusting of snowfall. Little of the snow stuck on the city streets, but the nearby mountaintops received a new coating.

Downtown Los Angeles, California, has mostly warm, dry weather. In January, average daily temperatures range from about 48°F to 68°F (9°C to 20°C). Still, every once in a great while, the city gets a bit of surprise snow.

THAT'S A FACT!

Before February 2019, the last time it snowed in downtown Los Angeles was January 1962. That was only a dusting as well. The last time the city received measurable snow was in 1949.

SNOW WAY!

Death Valley in southeastern California is one of the hottest places in the United States and the world. It's also one of the driest places in North America. So, it seems unbelievable that this area could ever have seen snowfall.

The snow recorded in January 1922 at Death Valley likely fell during the early morning hours. Temperatures were likely above freezing, but **evaporation** may have cooled the air enough to cause the snow.

Surprise—it has! It's usually only a trace, or very small, amount, but **meteorologists** have recorded snow in Death Valley a few times, all in January, including in 1949, 1962, and 1974. In 1922, meteorologists recorded 0.5 inches (1.3 cm) of snow on January 29.

The highest air temperature ever recorded in Death Valley (and in the world) was 134°F (56.7°C) on July 10, 1913.

The snow line is the place on a mountain above which there is always snow. This line mostly depends on how tall the mountain is and how close it is to the **equator.**

Windward and Leeward

1. Air currents hit the windward side of a mountain and are forced to flow upward.
2. This makes the air cool and form clouds. If there's enough moisture, precipitation forms.
3. If it's cold enough, that precipitation is snow.
4. The air that flows down the leeward side is much warmer and drier.

A MATTER OF ALTITUDE

When you think of Hawaii, you likely picture palm trees and sunny beaches, not snow. But it does snow in **tropical** Hawaii—if you know where to look! Places that are at a higher elevation (height above sea level) are more likely to get snow. The tops of the islands' tallest **volcanoes**, Mauna Kea and Mauna Loa, are regularly covered in it.

There are a few reasons **altitude** affects snowfall. The higher you go, the thinner the **atmosphere** gets. It can't hold heat as well. There's also more moisture in the air to fall as snow.

Mountains can also have a major effect on their surroundings' snowfall. They have a windward side, or a side the wind hits, and a leeward side, or a side that is protected from the wind.

SNOWY...FLORIDA?

In general, places closer to the equator have warmer **climates**. This is because these places get more direct light and heat from the sun. The southernmost point of the U.S. state of Florida is only about 1,700 miles (2,735.9 km) from the equator. So, it seems like southern Florida would never see snow. Right?

Well, snow is uncommon there. But in January 1977, southern Florida was surprised by snow **flurries** as far south as the city of Homestead.

Miami, about 30 miles (48.3 km) northeast of Homestead, also received some snowfall in January 1977.

THAT'S A FACT!

No snow has ever been recorded in Key West, the continental United States' southernmost city. The 1977 Homestead snowfall is still the southernmost snowfall ever noted in the continental United States.

DEALING WITH IT

People in snowier climates may laugh at the idea of a sprinkling of snow causing problems in other places. However, if people don't usually have to worry about snow, they might not have good ways to deal with it!

Cars are lined up on a road during an uncommon snowfall in Birmingham, Alabama, in 2015.

While northern communities may have many snowplows to deal with wintry weather, southern communities might have only a few—or none! People may not be used to driving in snow. Schools might not have extra class days planned in case of snow days.

THAT'S A FACT!

Some spots in the Northeast get lake-effect snow. This happens when cold air moves over the warmer waters of a lake. The air picks up water vapor, which rises, cools, and forms bands of clouds full of snow.

CLIMATE CHANGE

Increased snowfall—and snowfall in places that don't usually get it—can be a sign of climate change. This is the long-term change in Earth's climate, caused partly by human actions such as burning oil and natural gas.

When some people think of climate change, they think of global warming. So, how can more snow be a sign of a warmer world? There are a few reasons, but one is that the warmer planet means more moisture evaporates into the atmosphere.

Cars give off gases that make climate change worse. Combining trips and sharing rides can help.

GLOSSARY

altitude: Height above sea level.

atmosphere: The mixture of gases that surround a planet.

climate: The average weather conditions of a place over a period of time.

continent: One of Earth's seven great landmasses.

equator: An imaginary line around Earth that is the same distance from the North and South Poles.

evaporation: The act of changing from a liquid to a gas.

flurry: A light, brief snowfall.

meteorologist: Someone who studies weather, climate, and the atmosphere.

precipitation: Rain, snow, sleet, or hail.

temperature: How hot or cold something is.

tropical: Having to do with the warm parts of Earth near the equator.

volcano: An opening in a planet's surface through which hot, liquid rock sometimes flows.

FOR MORE INFORMATION

Books

Drimmer, Stephanie. *Ultimate Weatherpedia: The Most Complete Weather Reference Ever.* Washington, DC: National Geographic, 2019.

Jacoby, Jenny. *STEM Starters for Kids: Meteorology Activity Book.* New York, NY: Racehorse for Young Readers, 2019.

Noonan, Jim. *Professor Figgy's Weather and Climate Science Lab for Kids.* Beverly, MA: Quarry Books, 2022.

Websites

Grow Your Own Snow

kids.nationalgeographic.com/books/article/make-snow
National Geographic Kids offers instructions for a fun, easy snow science experiment.

A Guide to Climate Change for Kids

climatekids.nasa.gov/kids-guide-to-climate-change
NASA Climate Kids provides this look at climate change and how kids can help fight it.

Where Does It Snow the Most?

wonderopolis.org/wonder/where-does-it-snow-the-most
Learn more about what locations get the most snow on this Wonderopolis page.

Publisher's note to educators and parents: Our editors have carefully reviewed these websites to ensure that they are suitable for students. Many websites change frequently, however, and we cannot guarantee that a site's future contents will continue to meet our high standards of quality and educational value. Be advised that students should be closely supervised whenever they access the internet.

INDEX